the guide to owning an
Ocicat

Bill McKee

Photo: Isabelle Francais

© T.F.H. Publications, Inc.

Distributed in the UNITED STATES to the Pet Trade by T.F.H. Publications, Inc., 1 TFH Plaza, Neptune City, NJ 07753; on the Internet at www.tfh.com; in CANADA by Rolf C. Hagen Inc., 3225 Sartelon St., Montreal, Quebec H4R 1E8; Pet Trade by H & L Pet Supplies Inc., 27 Kingston Crescent, Kitchener, Ontario N2B 2T6; in ENGLAND by T.F.H. Publications, PO Box 74, Havant PO9 5TT; in AUSTRALIA AND THE SOUTH PACIFIC by T.F.H. (Australia), Pty. Ltd., Box 149, Brookvale 2100 N.S.W., Australia; in NEW ZEALAND by Brooklands Aquarium Ltd., 5 McGiven Drive, New Plymouth, RD1 New Zealand; in SOUTH AFRICA by Rolf C. Hagen S.A. (PTY.) LTD., P.O. Box 201199, Durban North 4016, South Africa; in JAPAN by T.F.H. Publications. Published by T.F.H. Publications, Inc.

**MANUFACTURED IN THE
UNITED STATES OF AMERICA
BY T.F.H. PUBLICATIONS, INC.**

Contents

The publisher thanks the following owners of cats pictured in this book: Patricia Clarke, Trudy Cline, Virginia Daly, Diane Dunn, Dot and Bob Ehlers, Madeleine Ewald and Sandy Duncan, Rebecca Clifton Garvin, Victoria Garvin, Louis and Maricava Johnson, Oliver H. Jones, Pamela and David Julian, A. D. Lawrence, Kelly Mayo and Lee Hov, Bill McKee, Mary Morea, Rebecca-Nan, Nancy and Gerry Payne, June Shatto, Lisa Kuzara Siebold, Gwen van Toorenenbergen, and Julie Williams.

Special thanks to Sonja Moscoffian

Photo: Isabelle Francais

History of the Ocicat

The Ocicat is a relatively new breed with beginnings in the 1960s. It was first bred by Mrs. Virginia Daly of Dalai Cattery in Michigan. Mrs. Daly's daughter (also named Virginia) thought that this new spotted cat looked like an ocelot and gave the breed the name (originally spelled "OciCat") that has stuck to this day. Mrs. Daly referred to what we now call spots as "dots," to distinguish them from other white markings that were then called spots. As the breed has become more widely known, these terms have evolved, and we now refer to the Ocicat as "spotted." Today, the Ocicat is recognized as the domestic feline breed that most closely mimics the spotted cats of the wild.

The first Ocicat breeding was a surprise, or as Mrs. Daly put it, "a gift." Mrs. Daly intended to produce an Aby-pointed Siamese by mating an Abyssinian with a Siamese, then breeding the result back to the Siamese. However, along with the sought-after Aby-point kittens came a unique, spotted kitten.

Tonga, the first spotted Ocicat, was sold as a pet for $10 to a medical student named Thomas Brown with the agreement that Tonga should be neutered. As luck would have it, the local newspaper did an article on Tonga and his owner, and publicity about

Mrs. Virginia Daly of Dalai Cattery in Michigan is the founder of the Ocicat breed. She was known for her experimental feline breedings, including that which produced the red-point Siamese she is holding here.

this spotted cat became widespread. A noted geneticist, Dr. Clyde Keeler of the University of Georgia, wrote to Mrs. Daly that Tonga should be bred back to his mother, Dalai She, in hopes of producing a "reincarnation" of the legendary and extinct Spotted Fishing Cat of Egypt. (Perhaps he had not heard of the Egyptian Mau.) Because Tonga had already been neutered and this was impossible, Dalai She was mated again to Tonga's father, a Siamese named Champion Whitehead Elegant Sun. More little Ocikittens resulted, and the spotted Ocicats were once again established.

THE FIRST SHOW OCICAT

In the late 1950s and early '60s, there was an inclination to breed and exhibit the rare and exotic. Experimental matings were done, and many breeds and varieties were developed that are now commonplace.

There are probably no other breeds of cat (or dog, horse, or bird for that matter) that were able to exhibit the first of their kind ever produced. The Ocicat may be unique in this regard. In February 1965, Mrs. Virginia Daly took Tonga to the Detroit Persian Society, Inc.'s 41st CFA Championship Cat Show. This lovely cat was displayed on the cover of the show catalog.

Tonga was entered in the "Special Exhibit Class" with rare breeds and varieties not yet accepted for Championship status, such as an ivory-point Siamese (White Persian/Siamese crossed with pure Siamese); a Pinto Siamese (Siamese crossed with calico domestic shorthair/Siamese hybrid); a Tonkinese (Burmese crossed with Siamese); a Black Cambodian Lucky Cat (imported from Southeast Asia, where an ancient tradition holds that cats with many kinks in the tail bring luck to their owners); a Golden

A noted geneticist suggested that the first Ocicat might be the "reincarnation" of the legendary, extinct Spotted Fishing Cat of Egypt. *Photo: Isabelle Francais*

THE DETROIT PERSIAN SOCIETY, INC.

41st CFA Championship Cat Show

FEBRUARY 20-21, 1965

Benefit Anti-Cruelty and Michigan Humane Societies

"TONGA, THE OCICAT BY DALAI"

OWNED BY THE THOMAS BROWNS

PRICE 65c

In February 1965, Virginia Daly took Tonga, the first Ocicat, to the Detroit Persian Society, Inc.'s 41st CFA Championship Cat Show. He was featured on the show catalog cover.

American Shorthair cats were crossed with Ocicats to expand the gene pool. They added the gene for silver coats, as on this lovely Oci.
Photo: Isabelle Francais

Persian; a Havana Brown; a "long-haired Abyssinian" (now known as a Somali); a Russian Blue; and a blue-point Himalayan.

Mrs. Daly took her retinue of rare exhibits to the show, including Tonga (Siamese crossed with Abyssinian/Siamese hybrid), who was already said to be the reincarnation of the extinct Egyptian Spotted Fishing Cat featured in Egyptian art. Tonga's mother, Dalai She, (ruddy-coated Aby crossed with Siamese hybrid) was exhibited along with Dalai Pink Lace, an Abyssinian-pointed Siamese (pure Siamese crossed with Aby/Siamese hybrid), and a pair of lynx-point Siamese (tabby domestic crossed with Siamese hybrid). Mrs. Daly also showed the Pinto Siamese mentioned above, as well as a "Lavender" male (Havana Brown crossed with lilac-point Siamese).

This must have made quite a display, and undoubtedly the interest was high among those attending the show who had come to see what was new in the cat fancy. No doubt they got an eyeful. Predictably, many of these creations, including the Ocicat, have gone on to establish themselves as distinctive breeds in the cat fancy and with the public in general.

Because Mrs. Daly was vice president and show manager of the Detroit Persian Society, she often used photos of her cats in various advertisements in the show catalog. Tonga was often featured in the catalog, as was a photo showing a litter of eight Siamese kittens.

INCREASED POPULARITY

As word of the new breed spread, other breeders became involved, using cats not only from Mrs. Daly but from different bloodlines and following her original recipe of Abyssinian crossed with Siamese, then bred back to the Siamese. Although there is no solid proof, it is suspected that both the Abyssinian and Siamese genetics mask the spotted pattern. While the first generation is all-ticked like the Aby, a characteristic that is dominant, breeding back to the genetically recessive Siamese will "unmask," or exhibit, the spotted pattern.

While the Ocicat can be said to be a "new" breed, its heritage is ancient. Coming from the Abyssinian and Siamese, two of the cat fancy's oldest breeds, the Ocicat is indeed an aristocrat. With the American Shorthair, which was crossed with Ocicats and introduced the gene for silver, came a more democratic bloodline. While the Egyptian Mau and other varieties within breeds have their spotted cats, none were being bred in the 1960s especially to emulate the spotted wild cat. There have been numerous attempts to cross domestic cats with various wild felines, but few have been successful. Ocelots, margays, and other spotted wild cats not only lacked the temperament necessary for a pet, they were scarce and no longer being imported. Many people, however, were anxious to have a spotted feline companion, and the Ocicat fit the bill perfectly. The Ocicat is a big, athletic cat, and the breed standard suggests that it should continually be developed to emulate cats of the wild. In fact, in the early days of exhibition, many people were afraid to handle this powerful, exotic-looking cat, despite its easygoing temperament.

Ocicat breeding has had its ups and downs over the years. The Ocicat was on the verge of receiving Provisional Breed Status from the Cat Fanciers' Association (CFA) in 1966, the first step toward becoming an officially recognized breed. Unfortunately, Mrs. Daly had to abandon her breeding of Ocicats in order to care for her ailing aunt, who had come to live with her and Whitman Daly, her husband. While a few breeders continued to carry the flag for the Ocicat, the momentum did not fully recover until 1981, when an organization called Ocicats International was formed with 22 charter members. Their goal was to promote the Ocicat to Provisional status and on to Championship status. Mrs. Daly had always promoted registration with the CFA,

because it is the largest cat registry. Although other cat associations were already registering Ocicats, Ocicats International targeted the CFA for full breed recognition.

The CFA granted Provisional Breed status in 1986, allowing the Ocicat to be shown as a Miscellaneous Breed. The Ocicat was promoted to Championship status the following year (1987). From 1982 through 1999, some 10,583 Ocicats were registered with the CFA, with a total of 786 cats registered in 1999 (a 34 percent increase over the 15-year average). In the UK, 70 Ocicats were registered with the Governing Council of the Cat Fancy in 1998. Many more Ocicats have been shown and bred in other countries and in other associations worldwide.

The popularity of Ocicats grew quickly as news of the new breed spread. Here, noted judge Virginia Wolfe examines Dalai Golden Phoenix, owned and bred by Virginia Daly and an important sire in the breed.

The Ocicat Standard and Colors

THE WILD LOOK

It seems to be part of human nature to want to exist with the wild and exotic. Animal lovers are always looking for something different. While many attempts have been

Because of the expansive gene pool of the Ocicat, encompassing the Abyssinian, Siamese, and American Shorthair, there are 12 colors available in the breed. *Photo: Gerry Payne*

made to cross domestic cats with wild cats, few of those attempts have been successful.

This is due in part to the rarity of wild cats and to the fact that they do not breed easily, if at all, with domestics. It is not uncommon for a wild cat to attack or even kill the intended mate. Often, the resulting offspring of a successful mating are sterile because of chromosomal differences. Even offspring of successful pairings will exhibit the wild temperament of the non-domesticated parent. This makes them extremely undesirable as pets, particularly when they outgrow kittenhood.

No wild blood was ever used in breeding Ocicats. However, not only have breeders pursued the "look" of the wild, they have sought to develop a more beautifully spotted cat, with a range of color beyond what is typical in wild felines. Because of the expansive gene pool of the Ocicat, encompassing the Abyssinian, Siamese, and American Shorthair, there are 12 colors available in the breed. This makes the Ocicat

Although non-spotted Ocicats are still Ocicats, most breeders prefer to breed only the best spotted cats to each other in order to produce the best kittens. *Photo: Isabelle Francais*

particularly interesting to those looking for something that is unusual or even unique.

Looking as if it is ready to spring into action, the Ocicat's large, powerful, and athletic frame mimics what is necessary for its wild cousins' survival. The description in the official show standard of the breed clearly states that the Ocicat should come as close as possible to replicating cats of the wild, not only in its spotted pelt, but in its physical structure. This is one of the most important characteristics of the Ocicat breed.

NON-SPOTTED OCICATS

Because of the breed's broad genetic base, Ocicats can be produced that have a valid Ocicat pedigree but that do not necessarily display the unique spotted pattern. These are known as AOVs (Any Other Variety).

They are allowed to be bred, and the kittens may be registered. While there may be the occasional advantage to instilling certain characteristics by using AOVs in a breeding program, as Ocicat numbers grow, more and more people prefer to breed spotteds to spotteds. Some AOVs (Siamese-like pointed, classic tabbies, and solids) have recessive patterns that are passed on for generations if they are not selectively bred out of the line. Breeding the best spotted to the best spotted is a sound practice.

The AOVs, those lacking the typical spotted pattern, may be ticked like their Abyssinian ancestors or may have mackerel stripes. (Ticking, a pattern also known as agouti, is the result of light and dark-colored bands on the hair shafts, which produce a characteristic effect when they lie across each other.) The ticks and stripes are defined

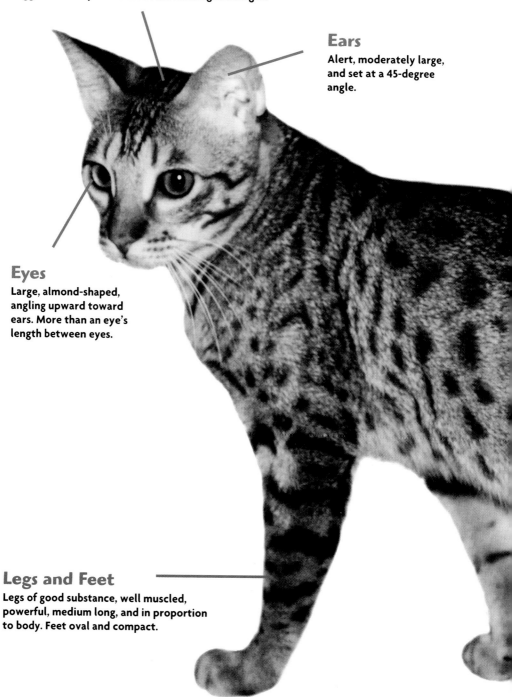

Head

Modified wedge, showing a slight curve from muzzle to cheek. Muzzle is broad and well defined, with a suggestion of squareness. Profile shows good length.

Ears

Alert, moderately large, and set at a 45-degree angle.

Eyes

Large, almond-shaped, angling upward toward ears. More than an eye's length between eyes.

Legs and Feet

Legs of good substance, well muscled, powerful, medium long, and in proportion to body. Feet oval and compact.

Torso

Solid, hard, rather long-bodied, with substantial bone and muscle. Athletic appearance, surprising weight for size. Never bulky or coarse.

Pattern

Spots scattered across shoulders and hindquarters and as far as possible down the legs. Large, well-scattered, thumbprint-shaped spots on sides of torso, with suggestion of spots circled by spots. Penalties for elongated spots.

Tail

Fairly long, somewhat slim, only a slight taper. Dark tip.

THE OCICAT STANDARD AND COLORS

as dominant genes, so it takes a ticked or striped parent to produce these types of kittens. Recessive genes can also be displayed if they are carried by both parents, even if the trait is not visible in the parents. These traits would include solid colors (which often show a "ghost pattern" of spots, as does a black leopard). Recessive genes also create points, a trait that limits color to the extremities. Points come from the color-restricting genes of the Siamese. Another recessive gene accounts for the classic (blotched) tabby, which shows a swirl of tabby pattern. It is generally believed that the randomness of the Ocicat's spotted pattern follows the swirl and horizontal pattern of the classic tabby. It was once believed that the classic tabby Ocicat could offer better pattern arrangement and that perhaps the solids could offer better contrast between spots and ground color. Because of this belief, breeders mated classics to solids. However, following the advice of geneticists, it appears that breeding the best spotteds to the best spotteds is the best practice today. Those breeders who have followed this routine have, in many instances, been able to breed most of the undesirable recessive characteristics out and to deselect the dominant genes from their lines.

While the AOVs have the typical Ocicat temperament and vigor, it is the beautifully spotted pelt that draws people to the breed. Those who do not care about the appearance and who want a lovely companion should consider these variants when they are available, because they are generally offered at a lower price. They are no less wonderful as pets.

THE OCICAT BREED STANDARD AND COLORS

This breed standard is recognized by the Cat Fanciers' Association (CFA), and it is reproduced here with permission. Note that Ocicats, like all breeds of cat, are judged according to how closely they meet the standard of perfection that is recognized by each association, rather than competing directly against the other cats on exhibition:

Point Score

Head (25)

Skull	5
Muzzle	10
Ears	5
Eyes	5

Body (25)

Torso	15
Legs and Feet	5
Tail	5

Coat and Color (25)

Texture	5
Coat Color	5
Contrast	10
Eye Color	5

Pattern (25)

General Description

The Ocicat is a medium to large, well-spotted agouti cat of moderate type. It displays the look of an athletic animal: well-muscled and solid, graceful and lithe, yet with a fullness of body and chest. It is alert to its surroundings and shows great vitality. There are 12 accepted Ocicat colors divided into 5 color classes, with all specimens possessing darker spots which appear in deep contrast to a lighter background.

The determining factor in answering any and all questions as to the correct color of an Ocicat will be the color of the tail tip without any comparison to the color of other body markings (see Ocicat colors). Each hair (except on the tip of tail) has several bands of color. It is where these bands fall together that a thumbprint-shaped spot is formed. This powerful, athletic, yet graceful spotted cat is particularly noted for its "wild" appearance.

HEAD: The skull is a modified wedge showing a slight curve from muzzle to cheek, with a visible, but gentle, rise from the bridge of the nose to the brow. The muzzle is broad and well defined with a suggestion of squareness, and in profile shows good length. The chin is strong and the jaw firm with a proper bite. The moderate whisker pinch is not too severe. The head is carried gracefully on an arching neck. An allowance is made for jowls on mature males.

EARS: Alert, moderately large, and set so as to corner the upper, outside dimensions of the head. If an imaginary horizontal line is drawn across the brow, the ears should be set at a 45-degree angle, i.e., neither too high nor too low. When they occur, ear tufts extending vertically from the tips of the ears are a bonus.

EYES: Large, almond shaped, and angling slightly upwards toward the ears with more than the length of an eye between the eyes.

TORSO: Solid, hard, rather long-bodied with depth and fullness, but never coarse. The Ocicat is a medium to large cat with substantial bone and muscle development, yet with an athletic appearance, and should have surprising weight for its size. There should be some depth of chest with ribs slightly sprung, the back is level to slightly higher in the rear, and the flank reasonably level. Preference is given to the athletic, powerful, and lithe, and objection taken to the bulky or coarse. It should be noted that females are generally smaller than males.

This chocolate spotted kitten, Pawaw's Envoyé of Shatori, displays the athletic prowess called for in the Ocicat standard. *Photo: Isabelle Francais*

The head of an Ocicat should be a modified wedge shape with a slight curve from muzzle to cheek. Pictured is Ch. Michon British Sterling. *Photo: Isabelle Francais*

THE GUIDE TO OWNING AN OCICAT

The overall structure and quality of this cat should be of greater consideration than mere size alone.

LEGS AND FEET: Legs should be of good substance and well-muscled, medium long, powerful and in good proportion to the body. Feet should be oval and compact with five toes in front and four in back, with size in proportion to legs.

TAIL: Fairly long, medium-slim with only a slight taper and with a dark tip.

COAT TEXTURE: Short, smooth and satiny in texture with a lustrous sheen. Tight, close-lying and sleek, yet long enough to accommodate the necessary bands of color. There should be no suggestion of wooliness.

TICKING: All hairs except the tip of the tail are banded. Within the markings, hairs are tipped with a darker color, while hairs in the ground color are tipped with a lighter color.

COAT COLOR: All colors should be clear and pleasing. The lightest color is usually found on the face around the eyes, and on the chin and lower jaw. The darkest color is found on the tip of the tail. Contrast is scored separately.

CONTRAST: Distinctive markings should be clearly seen from any orientation. Those on the face, legs, and tail may be darker than those on the torso. Ground color may be darker on the saddle and lighter on the underside, chin and lower jaw. Penalties should be given if spotting is faint or blurred, though it must be remembered that pale colors will show less contrast than darker ones.

EYE COLOR: All eye colors except blue are accepted. There is no correspondence

Cinnamon (top) and tawny (bottom) are just 2 of the 12 Ocicat color patterns. *Photo: Lisa Kuzara Seibold*

between eye color and coat color. Depth of color is preferred.

PATTERN: There is an intricate tabby "M" on the forehead, with markings extending up over the head between the ears and breaking into small spots on the lower neck and shoulders. Mascara markings are found around the eyes and on cheeks. Rows of round spots run along the spine from shoulder blades to tail. The tail has horizontal brush strokes down the top, ideally alternating with spots, and a dark tip. Spots are scattered across the shoulders and hindquarters, extending as far as possible down the legs. There are broken bracelets on the lower legs and broken necklaces at the throat—the more broken the better. Large, well-scattered, thumbprint-shaped spots appear on the sides of the torso, with a subtle suggestion of a classic tabby pattern: a spot circled by spots in place of the bull's eye. The belly is also well spotted. The eyes are rimmed with the darkest coat color and surrounded by the lightest color. Penalties should be given for elongated spots following a mackerel pattern.

DISQUALIFY: White locket or spotting or white anywhere other than around eyes, nostrils, chin and upper throat (except with agouti ground in silvered colors). Kinked or otherwise deformed tail. Blue eyes. Incorrect number of toes. Long hair. Due to the spotted patched tabby (torbie) cats resulting from the sex-linked O gene, no reds, creams, or torbies are allowed. Very rufous cinnamons and fawns may resemble red or cream, but never produce female torbies.

As on this chocolate spotted Ocicat, there should be an intricate tabby "M" on the forehead. Spots are scattered across the shoulders and hindquarters. *Photo: Isabelle Francais*

Ocicat Colors

TAWNY (brown spotted tabby): Black or dark brown spotting on a ruddy or bronze agouti ground. *Nose leather:* brick red rimmed with black. *Paw pads:* black or seal. *Tail tip:* black.

CHOCOLATE: Chocolate spotting on a warm ivory agouti ground. *Nose leather:* pink rimmed with chocolate. *Paw pads:* chocolate-pink. *Tail tip:* chocolate.

CINNAMON: Cinnamon spotting on a warm ivory agouti ground. *Nose leather:* pink rimmed with cinnamon. *Paw pads:* pink or rose. *Tail tip:* cinnamon.

BLUE: Blue spotting on a pale blue or buff agouti ground. *Nose leather:* pink rimmed with dark blue. *Paw pads:* blue. *Tail tip:* blue.

LAVENDER: Lavender spotting on a pale buff or ivory agouti ground. *Nose leather:* pink rimmed with dark lavender. *Paw pads:* lavender or pink. *Tail tip:* lavender.

EBONY SILVER: Black spotting on a pale silver/white agouti ground. *Nose leather:* brick red rimmed with black. *Paw pads:* black. *Tail tip:* black.

CHOCOLATE SILVER: Chocolate spotting on a white agouti ground. *Nose leather:* pink rimmed with chocolate. *Paw pads:* chocolate-pink. *Tail tip:* chocolate.

CINNAMON SILVER: Cinnamon spotting on a white agouti ground. *Nose leather:* pink rimmed with cinnamon. *Paw pads:* pink or rose. *Tail tip:* cinnamon.

BLUE SILVER: Blue spotting on a white agouti ground. *Nose leather:* pink rimmed with dark blue. *Paw pads:* blue. *Tail tip:* blue.

LAVENDER SILVER: Lavender spotting on a white agouti ground. *Nose leather:* pink rimmed with dark lavender. *Paw pads:* lavender-pink. *Tail tip:* lavender.

FAWN SILVER: Fawn spotting on a white agouti ground. *Nose leather:* pink rimmed with fawn. *Paw pads:* pink. *Tail tip:* fawn.

This Ocikitten is a cinnamon silver, one of the least common Ocicat colors.

Ch. Robin Cliff Fawne of Ay Shaka is a fawn silver Ocicat. *Above and below: Isabelle Francais*

The Ocicat Temperament

To understand the character of the Ocicat, one has to appreciate the changes that have occurred in its ancestral breeds (Siamese and Abyssinian) over the past 30 years or so. The Siamese of yesteryear was a larger and more easygoing cat than the lithe and kinetic Siamese we see today on the show table. The same can also be said for the Abyssinian, because breeders have emphasized color and breed type along with other attributes in this breed. Like its Siamese and Aby ancestors, the Ocicat retains its kitten-like playfulness into adulthood. It is, however, somewhat less rambunctious than these two other breeds, and in its laid-back personality it is perhaps

Characteristics of the Siamese, Abyssinian, and American Shorthair cat breeds have all come together to form the Ocicat temperament. *All photos: Isabelle Francais*

Like its Siamese and Aby ancestors, the Ocicat retains its kitten-like playfulness into adulthood.
Photo: A. D. Lawrence

more in keeping with the American Shorthair.

The breed standard describes the Ocicat's physical stature as "moderate," and the same can be said for its temperament. Many have described the Ocicat as being somewhat dog-like, in that it aims to please its master and often recognizes its own name. The Ocicat generally comes when called and loves to retrieve balls and toys. In fact, an Ocicat will often bring toys to her owner to begin a game. Ocicats take to walking on a leash with little training, and they love to go for rides in the car if accustomed to it. Some Ocicats seem to be fascinated with water, and they will follow their owner into the bathroom to watch her bathe. Few felines actually enjoy being bathed, but the Ocicat seems not to resent it as much as most.

Like many Ocicats, this blue cat has taken to walking on a leash with little training.
Photo: Bill McKee

Most breeders ask that Ocicats be kept indoors in deference to cars, disease, and interactions with wild animals. *Photo: Madeleine Ewald*

Ocicats are very adaptable and make themselves at home in almost any situation to which they have been introduced properly. As with any animal, there are personality differences among individuals. A houseful of "Ocies" will show an array of distinct temperaments.

Because the Ocicat represents a heritage of three separate breeds, the pitfalls of inbreeding have, for the most part, been avoided. Some credit the attribute of "hybrid vigor" to the Ocicat's size and hardiness. Queens usually give birth easily and produce large litters that they care for readily. It is not unusual for the females to seek human company when birthing, and neither sex is shy about breeding in front of an audience. Two queens that give birth at the same time

Ocicat queens like GC Galax Moon Dancer of Tesserae usually give birth easily and produce large litters that they care for readily. *Photo: Isabelle Francais*

may even share their kittens with each other, the way lionesses do.

Ocicats become more sedate as they mature, as do most cats, but they still retain their athletic prowess and energy into adulthood. They are excellent hunters and mousers and should be housed indoors to protect the local bird and rodent populations. Like a dog, they will bring these animals into the house if given the opportunity, so that the owner can see and appreciate their hunting abilities. Because diseases can be transmitted in this way—to say nothing of the impact this has on nature—it is not a good idea to let your cats roam and hunt. Most breeders ask that Ocicats be maintained as an indoor animal in deference to cars, disease, and interactions with wild animals.

Despite their wild appearance and regal bearing, Ocicats are very affectionate and want to please their owners. *Photo: Isabelle Francais*

With consistent reinforcement, Ocicats can *usually* be trained to stay off of counter tops and furniture. *Photo: Isabelle Francais*

Ocicats are not unusually vocal, and those who are looking for a quiet cat may find that Ocies are a good choice. *Photo: Isabelle Francais*

THE GUIDE TO OWNING AN OCICAT

Being shorthairs, Ocicats require little grooming. Perhaps because they come from such a broad genetic base, they are not finicky or picky but are rather easygoing in their dietary preferences. They will eat whatever is provided and are happy in most situations.

Unlike some breeds, Ocicats are content living with other animals. They get along with dogs, other cats of any breed, birds (large ones, that is, because they will try to hunt smaller birds and will tease them constantly), horses, etc. Were it not for the inherent and obvious dangers, Ocicats would be quite content living outside on a farm.

Although regal and elegant, carrying themselves much like a leopard or cheetah, Ocicats are very tractable and want to please their owners. They take scolding very seriously and, although they are not overly sensitive, they should not be constantly reprimanded. They know when they have made a mistake and, with consistent reinforcement, can usually be trained to stay off kitchen counters or to apply other rules of the household.

Ocicats are not aloof, and most act like they have never met a stranger. As with any breed, there are exceptions; personalities vary from one individual to another. Yet it can be said that Ocicats are generally secure, outgoing, and personable, as well as easy to train.

Ocicats are not unusually vocal. Queens in season are, of course, an exception. All cats vocalize from time to time and some Ocicats are encouraged to "talk" to their owners, but if you are looking for a relatively quiet cat, the Ocicat is a good choice.

Neither is the Ocicat a particularly mischievous breed. Ocicats do not look for trouble. You won't find them romping on the bookcase or climbing the curtains just to get attention. It is not uncommon, however, to find your Ocicat making a mad dash through the house in a spurt of crazed energy, either to get attention or simply to exercise.

People looking for a quiet, playful but not overly rambunctious, intelligent, easily trained companion that gets along well with other animals and strangers would do well to consider the Ocicat. This exotic, wild-looking feline is the cat world's answer to man's best friend.

Ocicats and kittens love to play with all kinds of store-bought and homemade cat toys.
Photo: Isabelle Francais

Selecting an Ocicat

If you wish to show or breed an Ocicat, you should thoroughly understand the breed standard. The cat you purchase should exhibit as many of the qualities in the standard as possible. The temperament is also very important and should not be overlooked. While no cat is absolutely perfect, one should always try to breed the best to the best and hope for the best. With a little luck and much effort, beautiful and "correct" kittens should result.

A SHOW-QUALITY OCICAT

If showing cats is your goal, you should

Determining which kittens in a litter are show quality, breeding quality, or pet quality requires a practiced eye. *Photo: Isabelle Francais*

If showing cats like GRC Megadots Uno is your goal, you should purchase from a reputable breeder the very best cat or kitten that you can afford. *Photo: Isabelle Francais*

Be very discriminating when selecting a cat for breeding purposes. Ideally, the cat should be of good show quality and should have a title or two before being bred. *Photo: Lisa Kuzara Seibold*

purchase from a reputable breeder the very best cat or kitten that you can afford. Cats of show quality are not inexpensive, and neither is the sport, so give consideration to the various aspects before committing yourself to a top-quality cat or kitten. You should educate yourself thoroughly to avoid disappointment. It is also unfair to procure a show cat and not be able to follow through, because many breeders expect their top cats to be shown and may even stipulate this in their sales contract.

AN OCICAT FOR BREEDING
You should be as discriminating as possible when selecting a cat for breeding purposes. Ideally, the cat should be of good show quality and should have a title or two before being bred. Having a cat that has won the title of Grand Champion is very helpful in finding good homes for the kittens.

Networking through people who show cats is a very good way of finding proper cats for breeding as well as for finding homes for kittens. It is possible to breed good-quality kittens even if one or both parents possesses a flaw that would keep him or her from becoming a top competitor. However, if both parents exhibit the same shortcoming, it is a bit too much to hope that the kittens would not have the problem as well. The world is not short of cats, so investigate local ordinances and network with as many breeders and exhibitors as possible before deciding to breed.

A PET-QUALITY OCICAT
Selecting a beautiful and healthy pet is much easier. Be suspicious of anyone wanting to deliver the cat or kitten to you. While it may sometimes be necessary to have a cat shipped to you from a long

distance (very young kittens should never be shipped, however), it is always best to visit the breeder and determine if the kitten comes from an environment of which you approve. Accepting a kitten sight unseen is asking for trouble.

Do not be afraid to ask questions or ask for references. Breeders that are reluctant to provide either should be avoided. Raising cats is not especially lucrative, and those who are motivated by profit are usually doing so at the expense of their animals' welfare. But do expect to pay a fair price and know that quality can come with a significant price tag. Even a kitten found on the streets will cost the new owner quite a bit for a vet check, inoculations against feline diseases, and so forth.

A reputable breeder will have given a kitten her first shots at least and will make some health guarantees in the sales agreement. The kitten will also be well socialized and off to a good start before the breeder will let her go. To ensure a strong immune system and adequate littermate socialization, most breeders do not release a kitten until she is 12 to 16 weeks of age. It would be a mistake to introduce a new cat to a home that already houses felines without a period of quarantine and all possible preventive measures.

It is stressful for any cat to make a change into a new home, so it is very important to visit the kitten's environment before making a selection. This is the only way you can

It is always best to visit the breeder in person and determine if the kittens come from an environment of which you approve. (Note that the blue eyes of these kittens will change or darken with age.)
Photo: Lisa Kuzara Seibold

To ensure a strong immune system and adequate littermate socialization, most breeders will not sell a kitten until he or she is 12 to 16 weeks of age. These cinnamon and lavender kittens, pictured with their chocolate spotted mother, are just about the right age. *Photo: A. D. Lawrence*

judge the personality and temperament of the kitten properly as well as meet at least one, if not both, of the parents. A lot can be determined from evaluating the parents and other adults of the breed.

WHICH SEX TO PURCHASE?

When selecting an Ocicat for a pet with the intention of spaying or neutering him or her, it makes little difference whether you purchase a male (tom) or female (queen). Either sex will make an equally nice companion. Males, of course, are usually larger, and some people find this desirable. Some feel that males are somewhat more consistent and less moody than females. However, cats are individuals, and selecting a personality that suits your own is important. While an outgoing kitten may develop into a more sedate adult, you can tell a lot by evaluating a litter and noticing how the kittens interact. The bold and bossy will stand out, as will the shy recluse. The amount of attention and socialization the kittens receive also makes a big difference.

If you intend to show your cat, either male or female will do. There are plusses and minuses with both sexes: Females may be difficult to keep in top coat condition during estrus, for example, and males may protest the presence of other males caged nearby. The selection usually has more to do with the quality of cat that you seek. Again, it is best to purchase the finest cat available. The price for a top show-quality Ocicat can be significant, as can expenses for travel and everything else involved with exhibiting felines.

If you want to breed Ocicats, selecting a top-quality female would be the best move. Housing a whole (unneutered) male can be a considerable undertaking. Because whole toms spray urine to mark their territory, it is necessary either to keep them caged, have them wear stud pants (a sort of kitty diaper), or give them a room of their own. Their odor is very noticeable to those not used to it, and a space for them that can be easily disinfected is a must.

Females that have not been spayed come into estrus (heat) seasonally and call out for the attention of males. They, too, need to be housed separately from males to avoid unplanned matings.

Selecting a kitten with a personality that suits your own is important. *Photo: Isabelle Francais*

Aspiring breeders should be aware that housing a whole (unneutered) male is quite an undertaking. Here, Int. GC, RW Echoesofmaja Runs With Thunder models his stud pants, just one example of the necessary measures a breeder must take. *Photo: A. D. Lawrence*

Grooming and General Care

SUPPLIES AND EQUIPMENT

Supplies and equipment are necessary for owning any cat. There are many types of litter boxes on today's market, some quite sophisticated. Depending on your needs, even

Scratching posts and other cat furniture are essential if you want to avoid damage to sofa and curtains. *Photo: Isabelle Francais*

the simplest litter box will suffice as long as it is large enough to accommodate this large breed of cat. It is important that the litter be kept clean and changed as necessary.

Other essentials are scratching posts and cat furniture if you want to avoid damage to sofas and curtains. Scratching posts come in various shapes, sizes, and configurations, and some are quite elaborate. Choose those that fit into your situation and decor. If the post is placed in the right location, your Ocicat will quickly learn to use and appreciate the post and will leave more precious and forbidden items alone. Once you determine your Ocicat's favorite resting spots—the back of your velvet sofa, for example—place a small towel there to collect cat hair that can easily be removed and cleaned from time to time.

It is also a good idea to invest in a carrier, especially one that is airline-approved for shipping animals. The carrier can make a perfect bed for your Ocicat when she is at home and gives her a place that is safe and

Once you have determined your Ocicat's favorite resting spots, place a small towel or pillow there to collect cat hair. *Photo: Gwen van Toorenenbergen*

just for her. As much as your Oci might enjoy looking out the window while riding in the car, it is a good idea to transport her in her carrier. This provides her with a secure place if you are going to the vet's for a checkup, traveling on vacations, or making any other trips. Just imagine being in an automobile collision and having your cat injured in the accident or escaping onto the freeway. One never knows what accidents might happen.

You will need good-quality combs and brushes, even though your Oci is a short-haired cat. It is a good idea to use a fine-toothed flea comb from time to time to check for these pests, in order to get rid of them quickly if any are found. Fleas can be a nuisance and, at worst, can quickly debilitate small kittens. They also play a role in the life cycle of the tapeworm.

You will need food and water dishes as well as airtight/rodent-proof storage containers for food. A variety of balls and toys is also necessary to keep your Ocicat entertained and happy. One excellent place to get everything you need at prices that are competitive, if not cheaper, than other sources is at your local cat show.

SAFETY PRECAUTIONS

Before acquiring a new cat or kitten, there are certain hazards that need to be considered and, if necessary, corrected. Household dangers include electrical or

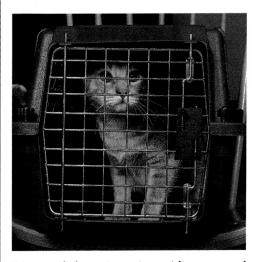

It is a good idea to invest in an airline-approved carrier for transporting your pet in the car. *Photo: Isabelle Francais*

A variety of balls and toys will be necessary to keep your Ocicat entertained and happy.
Photo: Isabelle Francais

extension cords that can be chewed, poisonous plants, chemicals, insecticides, open doors, windows without screens, and so on. It is not a good idea to allow your Ocicat outside unattended. There are many dangers outdoors, not the least of which are traffic, dogs, and even feral cats. Many locales have leash laws for cats as well as for dogs, and this practice is becoming more and more common. Be considerate and use good sense.

SLEEPING ARRANGEMENTS

Most cat owners do not object to their cats sleeping with them. Ocicats prefer to sleep with their owners whenever possible, if not under the covers, then right on the owners' pillows.

If this is objectionable, you should provide a cozy spot that the cat prefers. It is not

Throughout your Ocicat's life, keep potentially poisonous houseplants and flowers out of her reach.
Photo: A. D. Lawrence

Many Ocicats will be happy to curl up in a comfortable cat bed. *Photo: Lisa Kuzara Seibold*

unkind to place your cat in her carrier for the night, but Ocicats generally have the run of the house. As soon as you learn her preferred sleeping location, you can then place a cat bed or a small blanket in the spot she has chosen.

LITTER TRAINING

Ocicats are clean by nature and will always use the litter box if it is clean and located in a convenient spot. Like many domestic felines, some Ocicats do not like litter that is heavily scented. All kittens are trained by their mothers to use the litter box, so almost no training should be required. To begin training, you simply have to take the young kitten to the litter box when she awakens, after she eats, or after she plays. The kitten will soon get the idea. A kitten that turns in circles or searches in the corners may need to be shown where the litter box is. A few

words of praise when you see the kitten doing what she should be doing in the litter box are all that is necessary. If you notice your kitten making a mistake and eliminating where she shouldn't, quickly transfer her to the litter box with a scolding word, and offer much praise once you get her there. Don't make a big deal of a small mistake, and your kitten will soon be on the right track. Young kittens have limited control over bladder and bowels, so be attentive and help your kitten by making the litter box as clean and convenient as possible.

GENERAL TRAINING

Like most animals, cats live in the present. They only think about what is happening at the moment, so it is unfair and completely ineffective to call your cat only to discipline her for something she did yesterday or even several minutes before. All the cat will know is that she is being punished for coming when called. To be effective and avoid confusing the cat, you must reprimand her at the moment of the misdeed. If you see your Ocicat scratching the furniture, a simple "no" or clap of your hands is about all that is necessary. Overreacting because your cat scratched a precious heirloom rather than a ratty sofa means nothing to the cat (other than that her owner is making a big scene). It helps to praise your Ocicat for using the scratching post just as much as it does to scold her for using something that you consider inappropriate. Ocicats are smart and will soon learn the difference if you are consistent, observant, and dedicated to teaching the cat how to behave with good manners.

OCICATS AND OTHER PETS

Ocicats generally get along well with other animals, but they must be introduced properly, preferably at a young age. It is not smart to expect your Ocicat to get along with animals she naturally considers to be prey, such as small birds and rodents. While your cat may not immediately kill them, she will surely frighten or even maul them. When introducing your cat to a dog, be observant and be sure the two can be trusted before ever leaving them alone unattended. Dogs especially look to their masters for guidance and may do something to a cat when you are not present that they would never do if you were there.

Introductions to other cats should also be made cautiously and under supervision.

All kittens are trained by their mothers to use the litter box, so almost no training on the owner's part is usually required. *Photo: Isabelle Francais*

It is not smart to expect your Ocicat to get along with animals she naturally considers to be prey. Supervise such encounters with extreme care. *Photo: A. D. Lawrence*

A new kitten might do best if she is placed in a room by herself—in the bathroom, for example—so that for the first few days she can get used to the smells and sounds of the house and other animals before face-to-face introductions are made. It is better to take a little time and do things right than to have to overcome fear and trauma. Also, it is important to praise and lavish affection on the resident pets so that they do not become jealous of the newcomer that is receiving all the attention.

GROOMING

Being short-haired, Ocicats do not require the grooming that their long-haired cousins require. Even so, they should have their nails trimmed regularly, and they should be brushed to remove dead and loose hair. It is best to get them used to this at an early age;

If you begin clipping your kitten's claws when she is very young, she will not object to this procedure when she is older. *Photo: Isabelle Francais*

fussing over their nails before they need a trim will get them used to the idea of having them cut. As with any cat, it is better never to have an Ocicat declawed.

Go over the cat with a flea comb from time to time to check for parasites. A good brush is essential, and a rubber grooming glove is not a bad investment. But simply dampening your hands and going over the cat will remove any dead or loose hair and help prevent shedding all over the house. All cats shed, but you will notice heavy shedding when the seasons change. It is a good idea to give your cat a bath at this time (if no other), because bathing with a good shampoo not only cleans the cat but removes the loose hair and stimulates a healthy coat. Make whatever grooming you are doing pleasurable, and your cat will soon come to enjoy what might otherwise be a traumatic experience.

Take time during grooming and bathing to go over your cat to check her ears, teeth, skin, paws, and so forth. When bathing your Ocicat, it might be a good idea to have someone's help. Something as simple as dropping the shampoo on the floor can be a problem if you have a handful of wet kitty to deal with. Use a deep sink, if possible, or the bathtub, and always use warm, not hot, water. Soak the coat thoroughly before applying a shampoo formulated especially for cats. Rinse the shampoo and reapply a second time to ensure a thorough cleansing. It is extremely important to make sure that all shampoo has been rinsed out of the cat's coat before using a towel to dry the cat. Bathing should be done in a warm place so that chilling does not occur. Many cats get used to being dried with a hair dryer, but the noise can alarm some, and you must use caution not to overheat the animal.

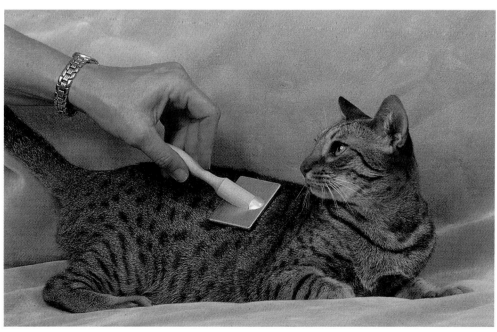

Purchase a good brush and use it on your Ocicat regularly to remove dead and loose hair.
Photo: Isabelle Francais

HANDLING CATS

As with all feline breeds, it is important that Ocikittens be handled and socialized at an early age. They should not, however, be introduced to cats outside the household until they have been fully inoculated against feline diseases.

If you have children, it is most important that they are instructed in the correct way to handle and appreciate their new pet. First of all, the kitten's privacy must be respected. Never let children wake up a sleeping kitten, because the kitty needs her sleep just as children do. Never let children play too roughly with a kitten or for an extended period of time. Cats like to play in short bursts. Always be sure that children never place elastic bands or string around the neck of a kitten, and never allow children to engage in a pulling match when a kitty has hold of a piece of string. The string could get caught on the cat's fragile teeth and damage them or even pull one out.

The correct way to lift a kitten is to place your hand underneath her chest. You may then place your free hand on her neck, throat, or shoulders to secure it. The cat may now be lifted and firmly but gently held to your chest while the hand securing the neck will be free to stroke the cat. A kitten or cat must never be lifted by her front legs or by the loose fur on her neck. When placing a kitten back on the floor, be sure she is held securely until she is at ground level. If she feels insecure, she will try to jump. In the process, she could scratch you or land awkwardly and hurt herself.

Take time during grooming to go over your cat carefully, checking and cleaning the eyes, ears, skin, and so forth as necessary.

Never allow a kitten or cat's hindquarters to dangle when you lift her. Place one hand underneath the chest, and as you lift, slide the other hand underneath the back legs to support them. *Above and below: Isabelle Francais*

Feeding Your Ocicat

Generally speaking, Ocicats are not finicky eaters. Even fussy cats will not allow themselves to starve in most cases, no matter how much they detest a particular brand of food.

Kittens, on the other hand, may require some patience and supervision to get them on the road to healthful eating habits. While adults can subsist on one or two daily meals, kittens, with their smaller stomachs and growing appetites, require several small meals each day.

There are many commercial cat foods on the market and much debate as to which is best. Follow the advice of the person from whom you acquired your cat or kitten. Your

There are many commercial cat foods on the market and much debate as to which is best. Follow the advice of your breeder and veterinarian. *Photo: Isabelle Francais*

Kittens must be fed several small meals daily. *Photo: Isabelle Francais*

veterinarian can also suggest a good diet. If a change in diet is required, do it slowly over the course of a few days to avoid an upset stomach.

Dry food has the advantage of not spoiling quickly, so it may be left out for your pet at all times. It is advisable to monitor the amount your cat is consuming. This can be difficult if several cats are allowed to eat together.

Moist food spoils quickly, so provide just enough to be consumed in a short period of time. Trial and error will tell you how much your cat will eat. Note that kittens will consume larger portions and at longer intervals as they grow. Any leftovers should be refrigerated and discarded after 24 hours. Prepare fresh meals daily.

Remember that cats are carnivores. In the wild, cats are predatory and eat the flesh of other small animals. In so doing they consume bone, internal organs, and muscle meats, along with a small amount of vegetable matter from the stomachs of their prey. Keep this in mind when preparing food for your cat, and give her a variety of well-cooked meats. If your cat will eat vegetables, cook them to imitate partial digestion. Human foods such as cookies and chips are not appropriate for cats, no matter how much they want them.

COMMERCIAL FOODS

Many commercial foods are available and may be dry, semi-moist, or moist. Offering a variety is a good way to keep your cat interested and also helps ensure that she will get a range of nutrition if something is missing from a single food source. Commercial diets containing high amounts of vegetable protein or animal byproducts are not as good as those based on meats, poultry, and fish.

Making homemade cat food is only feasible if you have the time and knowledge and use foods of the same high quality that you would eat yourself. *Photo: Nancy Payne*

Dry food provides good exercise for teeth and jaw muscles and has the advantage of convenience. Because dry food contains very little water, an unlimited amount of clean, fresh water should be available at all times.

There is controversy as to whether or not to supplement the regular diet with vitamins, minerals, or enzymes. Over-supplementation can lead to problems, just as a deficient diet can. You should know what nutrition your cat is already getting before adding too many supplements.

PREPARING YOUR OWN FOOD

Making homemade cat food is only feasible if you have the time and knowledge and use foods of the same high quality that you would eat yourself. (There are also fresh-frozen commercial pet foods available.) Meats in a homemade diet may include beef, poultry, or lamb and should be boiled or cooked before being offered. Fish should be steamed or boiled, with whitefish preferred to sardines or tuna that have been canned in oil.

Cheese, egg yolks, pasta, and boiled rice help round out the diet and add variety. Some cats like a little bit of cooked vegetables, while others avoid greens altogether.

HOW MUCH TO FEED

Cats prefer to eat frequent small meals. Adults can manage with two meals or even one large meal per day, but they prefer to nibble throughout the day when possible. Offering dry food at all times along with small meals of canned food is a popular feeding method.

Kittens, on the other hand, must have several small meals daily. Until the kitten is 16 weeks old, she should be offered 4 meals per day. These can be decreased to 3 meals per day at 16 weeks, while still feeding the same or a little more in quantity. At about nine months of age, two meals per day becomes appropriate. A cat may remain on this schedule through adulthood.

Cats like a predictable schedule, so consistency is appreciated. Of utmost importance is that your feline gets a good, well-balanced, and clean diet in amounts suitable to her age and nutritional requirements.

Females in later stages of pregnancy or nursing should be fed like kittens. They should receive more meals and a diet richer in calcium and protein.

Ocicats have a tendency to become overweight as they mature, especially if they are spayed or neutered. This can become a problem and should be addressed by feeding them diets that are appropriate for older cats, such as the commercial dry foods that are marketed for "seniors."

WATER

It is essential that your Ocicat have fresh, clean water available at all times. Cleanliness is critical to good health, and therefore food and water dishes should be washed daily and disinfected regularly. A dilute solution of bleach works well if the dishes are allowed to soak in it for at least one hour and are then rinsed very well.

Water quality varies from region to region, and if you do not care for your local tap

Females in later stages of pregnancy or nursing should be fed like kittens. In other words, they need more food and a diet richer in calcium and protein than that of other adult cats. *Photo: A. D. Lawrence*

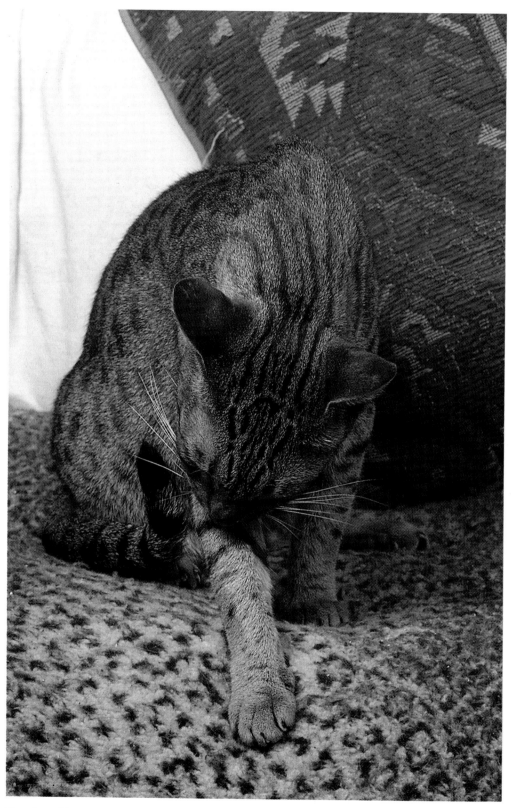

There's nothing more satisfying than a good bath after a good meal. *Photo: Isabelle Francais*

The stress of introducing a new cat into your home can cause behavioral as well as dietary changes in both the new arrival and the longtime inhabitants. *Photo: Isabelle Francais*

water yourself, chances are your cat won't, either. Bottled mineral water is a good alternative. Avoid distilled water, because it lacks some necessary minerals.

FEEDING THE NEW ARRIVAL

A move or change in environment stresses both kittens and adult cats. While adults are better able to cope with stress and may be able to go without food for several days, kittens cannot. Be on the alert for any changes of behavior, and be especially careful to ensure that the new arrival is getting the nutrition she needs. Tempting the new kitten with tasty treats is often necessary, but try not to upset her stomach with foods that are too rich or full of fat.

A change in diet can be upsetting to the digestive systems of adults and kittens alike. Ask the seller which food the cat is accustomed to, and keep the cat on the same diet. If a change in diet is necessary, make it gradually over a period of a few days.

New kittens may eat normally for a day or two and then, as the stress catches up to them, go off their feed. Dehydration is a serious concern, and water intake is critical. Tempt the kitten with watered-down, low-salt chicken broth. Moist foods are preferred to dry to ensure the kitten is getting the water she needs. Never feed any cat cow's milk, because it is not digestible to cats and can cause stomach problems.

Stress can trigger a viral problem that must be addressed quickly. Consult your vet if you have concerns. The vet may suggest treatment or a dietary supplement. Also, do not hesitate to contact the seller from whom you got the new arrival, because he or she may also have helpful advice.

Your Ocicat's Health

Just like any animal, your Ocicat can become the victim of numerous diseases and health conditions. It is not possible to suggest all the possibilities or cover all the remedies, but some general information is helpful.

Always purchase a healthy cat or kitten from someone you can trust. Visiting the home from which the animal comes will tell you a great deal about her general health and condition. Are the other cats in the household well and thriving? Are they provided with a safe and clean environment and nutritional diet? Is overcrowding a problem? Are all individuals given the space and attention they need?

Prevention and good animal husbandry are worthy investments and far preferable to costly treatments down the road. Let's review healthy management practices first.

HYGIENE

Make it a daily practice to follow a regimen of cleanliness and sound hygiene. Disease-causing organisms (called pathogens) can overwhelm your cat's immune system, so keeping these to a safe minimum is critical in maintaining good health.

Following these simple rules of good hygiene will put you on the road to maintaining a healthy Ocicat:

1. Any uneaten moist food should be stored in the refrigerator if you intend to offer it at a later time. Prepare fresh food daily and discard all leftovers at the end of the day.

2. Always use clean dishes and utensils that have been washed and handled as you would your own.

3. Fresh and moist foods should be stored in the refrigerator, and dry foods should be in airtight containers in a cool, dry place that is protected from rodents. Unopened canned foods have a longer shelf life than bagged dry foods. Check the processing date on the bag when purchasing your cat's food.

4. Always wash and/or disinfect your hands after handling someone else's cat. To

It's a dangerous world out there for your little Ocicat. Just like any animal, your cat can become the victim of numerous diseases and health conditions. *Photo: Isabelle Francais*

avoid bringing parasites home to your cats, change your shoes and clothing if you have visited the home of another cat owner.

5. Clean and disinfect your cat's litter box and provide clean litter routinely. Remove waste whenever you notice it. Cats can share litter boxes, but it is best to provide several if you have several cats. Look to see if the feces are normal or foul-smelling, and take immediate action if you notice anything unusual.

6. Groom your Ocicat often and inspect her for any injuries, pests, or abnormalities. Treatment for any ailments should begin immediately.

SPECIAL HEALTH CONCERNS FOR BREEDERS

For registration purposes, it is critical to know the parentage of the kittens. Breedings must be supervised so that one is certain of the father of the kittens. Knowing exactly when the mating takes place is helpful in order to predict when the kittens are to be born—approximately 63 days after mating—so that a quiet place can be prepared for the queen to give birth. Should things not go quite right, medical assistance or a C-section can be arranged.

It is very important to keep records on all cats in a breeding situation: immunization records, dates of birth on adults and kittens, numbers of kittens born (both live and stillborn), abnormalities, birth weights, etc. You will be surprised how easy it is to forget or to get confused. It is a good idea to keep a card file handy to write down anything pertaining to the cats, such as health or diet changes, heat cycles, or anything you may want to refer to in the future.

When feeding your cat, always use clean dishes and utensils that have been washed and handled as you would your own. *Photo: Dot and Bob Ehlers*

Clean and disinfect your cat's litter box routinely to ensure that she will continue to use it faithfully.
Photo: Diane Dunn

Breeders who are working with more than a few cats find it beneficial to house them in special quarters known as a cattery. This can simply be a room or rooms dedicated to various cats, or it may be a specially designed building suitable for the purpose. Most often, the males are housed separately from the females, and queens with kittens are given separate quarters as well. One must also be able to quarantine new arrivals to prevent the possible spread of disease and infections. Quarantine is important not only for newly acquired cats, but for outsiders brought in for breeding purposes if you choose to participate in this practice. Many breeders instead operate a "closed" cattery and forbid the introduction of any outsiders for any reason in order to avoid the risks of disease and infection.

Many precautions are taken at cat shows to avoid the spread of disease. Most show fliers specify that entries must be inoculated and free of disease. As a further precaution, judges disinfect their hands, toys, and the judging table in between handling entries. Show cages are cleaned and disinfected after each show. Even though most diseases now have vaccines that help prevent them, it is still important to take precautions whenever possible.

RECOGNIZING AN ILL CAT

Cats, like many animals, will try to hide an illness or injury. Take notice of anything unusual. You will need to distinguish between self-correcting conditions, like a sprain or pulled muscle or minor diarrhea, and more serious problems that might require a veterinarian's help. It is better to be safe than sorry, and it is much easier to treat an illness at its onset than to wait until it has advanced. Self-correcting conditions

Breeders who are working with more than a few cats find it beneficial to house them in special quarters known as a cattery. *Photo: A. D. Lawrence*

usually become better in 24 to 48 hours. Pay close attention, take the cat's temperature, and call your vet for advice if you are concerned. Some things that could indicate a problem are:

1. Foul-smelling or bloody diarrhea. Straining while defecating or urinating or the presence of blood in the urine indicates a problem that needs investigation and correction.

2. Any discharge from the eyes or nose should be assessed and, if it continues for more than a day or two, treated.

3. All cats vomit occasionally (if they have overeaten or consumed grass, for example), but repeated or continued vomiting is not normal.

4. Difficulty breathing or noticeable wheezing could indicate respiratory problems. These problems are often serious and must be treated.

5. Excessive grooming (licking or scratching) could indicate a problem. Check for wounds, fleas, or fungus.

6. Lesions, cuts, and bald spots should be treated.

7. Any dullness of coat or unusual loss of hair could indicate a problem.

8. A change in your cat's usual energy or attitude should be noted.

9. If the nictitating membrane (third eyelid) is clearly visible, if the eyes are glazed, or if you notice any weepiness, you should assume there is a problem. This could

be anything from a slight, temporary irritation to a very serious problem, so observe for a day or two and consult your vet if your cat needs treatment.

10. Note any change in your cat's eating habits.

11. Take note if the gums are red or swollen or if you notice any loose teeth. If the gums appear pale in color, it could indicate anemia or shock.

12. Any pain, obvious distress, or significant change in usual behavior indicates that your cat has a problem.

As an illness advances, the clinical signs become more numerous and more apparent. Any time a condition becomes worse instead of better, you should consider treatment.

DIAGNOSIS

Keep a written record of your cat's behavior. It can be helpful to know exactly when the first or last time a particular irregularity occurred.

A correct diagnosis must be made before treatment can be made. Many of the danger signs listed above are nonspecific and could be caused by any of a number of injuries or diseases. The advice of an expert should always be sought if you have any doubts about your diagnosis.

Stress is a significant cause of illness in cats, so be on the lookout for problems when you first get a new cat, when your cats have to travel, or when you are breeding your cats. Kittens especially can be affected

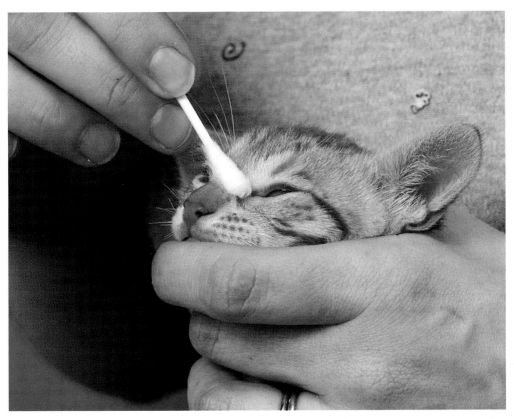

During regular grooming, note any discharge from the eyes or nose. If it continues for more than a day or two, it may require veterinary treatment. *Photo: Isabelle Francais*

by stress because their immune systems are not fully developed. Stress can compromise the immune systems of even an adult, and poor hygiene can lead to major problems.

If you decide that your cat needs to be seen by a veterinarian, transport your cat safely and warmly in a good cage or carrier. Take along your written notes of the signs, dates, and symptoms you've noticed, as well as a sample of feces and urine if at all possible. Some vets specialize in treating felines. By asking around, you should be able to find a vet that you can trust to be knowledgeable and astute in treating your Ocicat.

TREATMENT

Once a diagnosis is made and treatment prescribed, follow the directions thoroughly as you administer the medication or treatment. Do not discontinue giving medicine (especially antibiotics) simply because your cat is better, but follow through until all medication is given to ensure that the pathogens are killed and to prevent the cat from developing an immunity to the treatment if a relapse occurs.

VACCINATIONS

Some serious illnesses are extremely dangerous, and boosting the immune system with vaccines can prevent many of these illnesses. It is possible for your cat to contract these by simply breathing the air when other cats are present.

Before they are bred, females should be given shots to boost their immunity to make sure that plenty of antibodies are passed on to the kittens. A kitten receives antibodies and immune protection from colostrum, the substance her mother produces in the first few days of nursing. This protection may last for a few weeks or several months. It is recommended that you begin protecting the kitten with vaccinations beginning at six to eight weeks of age in order to be safe. Boosters should be given some weeks later and at regularly prescribed intervals to ensure protection.

If a cat survives a serious infectious disease, it is quite possible that the cat will be a carrier of that disease throughout her life. Therefore, all kittens should receive vaccination for the following diseases:

Rabies

Vaccines are effective in protecting domestic animals from this fatal disease. Unfortunately, the Center for Disease Control and Prevention reports an alarming rise and increased spread of rabies in wildlife. Rabies attacks the neurological system and destroys an animal's flight instinct, so beware of any wild animal that comes too close to your family and pets. Skunks, raccoons, bats, and foxes are not uncommon in urban areas, and all of these animals may carry rabies.

Rabies is not found in some isolated and island areas like Great Britain, Australia, New Zealand, Ireland, Holland, Sweden, Norway, and Hawaii. Quarantine laws are enforced in these places to prevent the introduction of this disease, and importation of cats and dogs is difficult.

Hawaii has relaxed its quarantine period if proof can be shown that the animal has a history of rabies vaccinations, and some cats and dogs may now be imported to the UK from Western Europe without quarantine under certain conditions.

Rabies is transmitted through saliva and can cause agitation, depression, muscle spasms, and paralysis leading to hallucinations, coma, and, eventually, death. Regular vaccinations prevent this disease.

Feline Panleukopenia

Known as feline distemper or enteritis, this is a highly contagious viral disease. Vaccinations should be given at about eight weeks of age, with a second booster following in four weeks and a third booster four weeks after that.

Feline Respiratory Disease

Known colloquially and incorrectly as "cat flu," feline respiratory disease encompasses a number of specific diseases. Two are especially dangerous: feline viral rhinotracheitis (FVR) and feline calicivirus (FVC). A combination vaccine is available and should be given when a kitten is six to eight weeks of age, followed by a booster four weeks later.

Feline Leukemia Virus (FeLV)

First diagnosed in 1964, this disease is actually more complex than the cancer of

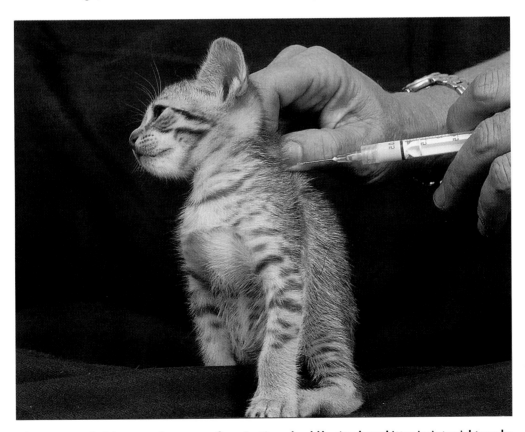

It is recommended that a regular course of vaccinations should begin when a kitten is six to eight weeks of age. *Photo: Isabelle Francais*

the blood that its name comes from. Feline leukemia weakens the cat's immune system, offering dangerous opportunities for other feline diseases. A vaccine for feline leukemia was developed in the mid-1980s.

FeLV is contained in saliva and is easily spread by cats licking each other or sharing food dishes. All breeding cats should be tested, and only those found negative should be vaccinated. The survival rate for those affected is about 70 percent, and these are considered carriers of the disease in most cases.

Feline Infectious Peritonitis (FIP)

This disease, which affects the cat's metabolism, is difficult to diagnose. However, intranasal liquid vaccines have proven effective and seem to reduce its development in the tissues of the nose.

PARASITES

There are both internal and external parasites that live off their hosts. Fleas, ticks, and lice are common external pests. While treatment is easily available and much more effective than in years past, repeated treatments are usually necessary to break the cycle of infestation.

Internal parasites are various species of worms and organisms that can debilitate and deteriorate the health of your cat. Roundworms are common and may be picked up from public parks or even your front yard. Keeping the litter box clean and your cat indoors will help prevent roundworms. Roundworms cause a loss of appetite, weight loss, and diarrhea.

Giardia is primarily transmitted through drinking water and can spread to humans. Symptoms such as diarrhea, mucus in the stool, dehydration, weight loss, depression, and decreased appetite are common. People can experience such symptoms as gastrointestinal inflammation, dehydration, and fatigue. Giardia can be difficult to diagnose but is easily treated once found.

Because internal parasites are so common, routine treatment is advised in kittens and in cats before they are bred. Periodic treatment should be discussed with your veterinarian.

SPAYING AND NEUTERING

Desexing your cat is advisable for several reasons ranging from population control, health concerns (including tumor prevention), to the modification of

One important sign of fleas, ticks, and lice in your Ocicat is excessive scratching and self-grooming.
Photo: Julie WIlliams

undesirable behaviors such as spraying. A female cat is normally spayed at about four months of age. Neutering (castrating) the male is done somewhat later. The operation is quite simple for the male and more complicated, yet very routine, for the female. While these operations may be performed at any age, it may take some time for adult cats (especially males) to modify or lose their habits of marking territory.

RINGWORM

It was once believed that tiny, circular worms burrowed into the skin and expanded outward to cause this disease. We now know ringworm is a fungal infection. Infected people or pets transmit ringworm through direct contact or environmental contamination. As the condition worsens, it creates a raised, red circle that spreads outward, often causing hair loss.

The most serious health problems associated with ringworm are infections caused by scratching. If you suspect ringworm, contact your vet, who will treat it with antifungal creams, shampoos, dips, and medications. Consider treating the cat's environment to prevent reinfection.

FIRST AID

When injuries occur, be prepared to deal quickly and effectively with the problem. Serious accidents usually happen if your cat escapes outside and is injured by a car, dog, or other cat. Traffic accidents are always serious and are often fatal. Bites and scratches from other animals are usually less destructive, but they do require immediate attention.

If your cat is hit by a car, place her on a board or other stiff object. Do not lift her head in case there is a spinal injury and also to prevent the aspiration of blood into the lungs. Keep your cat warm and quiet and talk soothingly as you take her to your vet or to emergency facilities. You may wrap the animal in a blanket or towel to restrict her movement and keep her warm.

Do the same for other serious injuries, and treat minor bites and scratches with antibiotic cream or ointments.

Consult your vet about insect bites as well as abscesses from bites and scratches, because topical ointments do little good.

Treat minor cuts by thoroughly washing and cleaning the area, cutting hair away if necessary, and applying an antiseptic. Serious bleeding should be pressure-bandaged around the body or leg to restrict the loss of blood.

Much is made of poisonous plants and other items, but cats are actually careful eaters and rarely swallow poisons. Even so, contact your vet and let him know what you suspect because various poisons require different treatments. Vomiting, for example, may be encouraged in one instance and not in another.

Trauma from attack or injury may not be immediately apparent, and your cat may go into shock at a later time. Be attentive and take your cat to the vet if she collapses, has pale gums, or shows other signs of shock. If you cannot get to a vet immediately, place your cat in a dark, quiet room and cover her with a blanket until you get instructions from your vet.

Exhibiting Ocicats

Since the first cat show in 1871 in London, England, shows and competitions have been at the center of the cat world. Serious breeders and fanciers live to show their cats, to socialize with others who share their interest, and to marvel at the best felines being produced. Shows are also the best place to see the wide variety of colors available in the Ocicat breed. They are usually the best and most affordable places to find the latest products and cat supplies.

People considering the purchase of an Ocicat should attend a show or two. Even if you are just looking for a pet to love and are not interested in showing or breeding, it is a good idea to see as many Ocicats as possible, consider the color possibilities, and get to know breeders. Kittens may sometimes be purchased at shows, but gaining information and getting to know the breeders is what is most important. A cat show usually has the newest and most complete selection of the supplies, toys, and equipment needed to make your new pet comfortable.

Knowing what a quality Ocicat looks like will save disappointment down the road. Many new owners believe that they don't care what their pet looks like, only to find themselves discouraged or even embarrassed as they get to know the breed and learn that their new pet looks hardly at all like the breed she represents.

THE SHOW-QUALITY OCICAT

A show-quality Ocicat must be a very good example of her breed. The male show cat must have two descended testicles, and all cats must have recent vaccinations and proper documentation. A show cat must be well socialized and used to being handled by strangers. A cat that bites or claws a judge may be disqualified from that ring. The more at ease and playful the cat is, the better her chances of advancement. Most judges, however, will be understanding and know that tension at a show runs high for cats and people alike.

Does your Ocicat have real star quality, like Ch. Telltail "Starbaby" of Megadots? A career in "show business" could be fun for both of you. *Photo: Dot and Bob Ehlers*

TYPES OF SHOWS

Cat shows may be large or small, but generally speaking, all breeds and most colors are represented. Some shows are organized for specialty competition featuring certain breeds or are designed for regional competition, with certain cats qualifying for larger national shows. The larger the show, the stronger the competition will be, with several national competitors usually present. Smaller shows, however, are a good place to begin and offer a chance for smaller competitors to pick up awards.

There are several organizations and associations that sponsor the shows, and their rules and procedures often vary slightly. But even the smallest show offers a chance to see many fine felines, with larger shows playing host to some of the best cats in the nation.

ENTERING A SHOW

Various cat magazines and newspapers will announce an upcoming show. Contact the secretary or entry clerk and return the entry form along with the required fees as stipulated for that show. It is important that you enter the correct class for your cat's age, sex, and color. Otherwise, your cat can be eliminated and the entry fees forfeited. The show secretary can offer advice if you need it.

SHOW SUPPLIES

You will need a variety of items for the show: a carrier, litter box, food and water dishes, blanket/small bed, grooming supplies, and decorations for the show pen. Bedding, curtains, toys, and other accoutrements should be new or at least clean in appearance.

Many people bring their own water as well as paper towels, disinfectant, a first aid kit, and medications. A veterinarian is always on call, if not actually present, for the event. You will also need your entry pass, vaccination or health certificates (if necessary), and whatever else the association requires. Because parking is not always convenient at shows, it is wise to invest in a cart to transport your equipment and supplies.

Make a checklist of your show supplies and go over it carefully before departing for the show. If you need to purchase something at the show, it's a good idea to do this before competition begins. Not only is there a better selection at the beginning of the day, but you'll find that things become hectic once the judging begins.

PREPARING YOUR OCICAT FOR THE SHOW

To do well in competition, your cat must be in his or her top form. Proper weight and muscle tone are essential. Only those cats that are in excellent condition will be winners at a competitive show.

Conditioning cannot be achieved overnight. Only cats that receive excellent diets, good health care, and plenty of exercise stand a chance of becoming strong contenders. Of course, much of the quality has to be in the genes to begin with, but quality care cannot be lacking in order to have a successful show career.

The day before a show should include a good bath as well as combing and grooming of the coat. Nails should be clipped and filed to make sure they won't accidentally scratch the judge. Make sure that the cat's ears and teeth are clean and that there are absolutely no fleas or other parasites. Your cat should look and feel the best she possibly can.

SHOW PENS

As you arrive at a show, you will be assigned a pen in which to place your cat. Usually, these are all-wire cages that have been cleaned and disinfected. Even so, some exhibitors choose to provide their own cage setup. Cages must be of a standard size and configuration but may vary in the materials from which they are constructed (wood, vinyl, etc). Some are quite elaborately decorated and may have air filtering systems and fans, which make the cats as comfortable and secure as possible. In Britain, however, the cages must be consistent, with no way of identifying the owners, because the judge moves around the hall from cage to cage. (In the US, the entries are removed from their pens and taken to each ring to be judged.)

Your show pen may be elaborately decorated or simply comfortable. Whatever its design, it will need to be draped on the back and sides for security and privacy. Plastic is often used as well as fabric, especially in the case of a whole male who may spray to mark his territory. Included in the cage should be a small, comfortable bed, a litter box, and dishes

A show cat like Ch. Dapajn Mojave, pictured with CFA Judge Craig Rothermel, must be well socialized and used to being handled by strangers. *Photo: Pamela and David Julian*

for water and food. Toys are also a nice addition, because your cat or kitten will be spending the day at the show.

COMPETITION AND JUDGING

Cat competitions and judging can be confusing to the newcomer. But all cat shows, regardless of registry affiliation or feline association, set up their shows in a similar manner.

Each show is made up of a number of separate and concurrently running "rings." Each ring is under the direct control of a judge who has spent numerous years in training. In each ring, there is usually a clerk who records the proceedings and a steward who makes sure each cage is ready for the next cat called to be judged.

Each cat or kitten is removed from her cage and placed on the table by the judge. Although in Britain the judging is done in private, in US exhibitions, an audience of owners and spectators is encouraged.

Category

Whether the individual cat is competing in the category of pedigreed Kitten, intact mature Adult (Championship), Alter/Premiership (male neuter or female spay), or Household Pet (non-pedigreed), each feline will be judged first in his or her appropriate competing category and then the specific division or color class. The judge handles the entries to assess coat condition, bone structure, weight, temperament, and other traits. A winning

Make a checklist of your show supplies and go over it carefully before departing for the show.
Photo: Pamela and David Julian

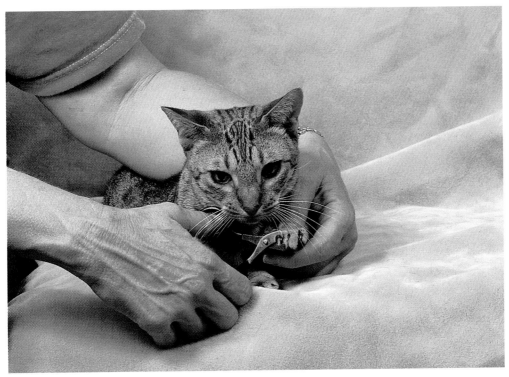

The day before a show should include a good bath, grooming, and claw-clipping for your Ocicat.
Photo: Isabelle Francais

cat is one that receives the highest total number of points.

Color and Division

Each recognized breed within a given registry or association has breed councils or committees that, with the approval of the governing body within the registry or association, determine the color (Blue, Chocolate, Ebony, Tawny, etc.) or the division (solid, tabby, shaded, sable, etc.) in which each feline of a specific breed may compete. In many breeds, the criteria that determine color or division are equally applied to short or long-haired varieties.

Sex

Normally, the males or females of each competitive category are also judged separately by sex, after which they compete for Best of Color or Best of Breed awards as a group.

Standards and Points

All cats (with the exception of Household Pets) are judged against a written standard rather than against other cats in competition. This standard may differ slightly from association to association, but in every instance it defines how a perfect example of a given breed should appear and behave. The standard must be precise enough for the judges to analyze and evaluate each cat accurately, while at the same time be flexible enough for changes over time.

A distinguishing characteristic of a breed (coat, head, ear, etc.) usually has more points assigned to it in the breed standard than points for other aspects of the cat. Judges frequently consult or even thoroughly memorize the breed standards. The ultimate goal of all serious breeders, regardless of registering affiliation or cat association, is to achieve the "perfect specimen" described by the breed standard.

AWARDS

The awards earned in each competitive category differ because of special characteristics of the cats at each competitive level. For instance, *Kitten* competition is for unaltered or altered pedigreed cats between certain age limits imposed by the rules of the governing registry or association. (The CFA Kitten competition is between the age of four and eight months.)

Championship competition is for unaltered pedigreed cats over the age of eight months and usually includes levels of achievement for previous show successes. In this category, a title such as "Open" represents a cat that has not yet been awarded sufficient wins to advance to the "Champion" level. In the CFA, for example, a Champion has six winners' ribbons. Once a cat is a Champion, the cat must defeat a set number of other cats in competition to claim the title of Grand Champion.

The *Premiership* competition is for altered, pedigreed cats over the age of

Some cat show exhibitors choose to decorate the wire cage provided at the show with elaborate draperies and furnishings. *Photo: Lisa Kuzara Seibold*

THE GUIDE TO OWNING AN OCICAT

An alternative to simply decorating the wire cage is bringing your own complete, unique cage setup to the show. *Photo: Lisa Kuzara Seibold*

Cat competitions and judging can seem disorganized and confusing to the newcomer, but you'll quickly become acclimated and feel like an old pro. *Photo: Isabelle Francais*

eight months. The titles follow a similar progression of Open, Premier, and Grand Premier. In some associations, other titles are possible, such as "Quad Champion" and "Supreme."

Household Pet competition is for all randomly bred or non-pedigreed domestic cats, In most associations, the cats must not be declawed, kittens must be at least four months of age on the opening day of the show, and all entries older than eight months must be neutered or spayed.

COMPETITIONS FOR NEW BREEDS

A Provisional or New Breeds and Colors category is a competition for breeds that have not yet achieved Championship status. In the CFA, this is the next-to-the-last step in achieving full breed recognition. Cats at this level of competition compete for color and breed wins only within their own breeds and do not compete against the recognized breeds for accumulated points or titles.

Miscellaneous competition is for those breeds not yet accepted for Provisional status but that have been accepted for registration and showing at the events of a given association. Cats shown in this class receive no awards of any kind, but the competition provides a means of introducing a new breed or color to the cat fancy, the officiating judges, and the general public.

CONCLUSION

Showing is time-consuming and costly, but for many it is a wonderful hobby and social event. It is wise to attend a couple of shows to familiarize yourself with the flow of the event and to avoid being unprepared. It is possible, however, to purchase everything you will need for exhibiting your cat at any of the larger shows where vendors are selling their wares.

THE GUIDE TO OWNING AN OCICAT

Cat Registry Associations

**American Association
of Cat Enthusiasts**
P.O. Box 213
Pine Brook, NJ 07058
Phone: 973-335-6717
Fax: 973-334-5834
E-mail: info@aaceinc.org
Web: www.aaceinc.org/
welcome.html

American Cat Fanciers Association
P.O. Box 203
Point Lookout, MO 65726
Phone: 417-334-5430
Fax: 417-334-5540
E-mail: info@acfacat.com
Web: acfacat.com

Australian Cat Federation (Inc)
Post Office Box 3305
Port Adelaide SA 5015
Phone: 08 8449 5880
Fax: 08 8242 2767
E-mail: acf@catlover.com
Web: www.acf.asn.au

Canadian Cat Association
220 Advance Blvd,
Suite 101
Brampton, Ontario
Canada L6T 4J5
Phone: 905-459-1481
Fax: 905-459-4023
E-mail: office@cca-afc.com
Web: www.cca-afc.com

The Cat Fanciers' Association, Inc.
P.O. Box 1005
Manasquan, NJ 08736-0805
Phone: 732-528-9797
Fax: 732-528-7391
E-mail: cfa@cfainc.org
Web: www.cfainc.org

Cat Fanciers Federation
P.O. Box 661
Gratis, OH 45330
Phone: 937-787-9009
Fax: 937-787-4290
E-mail: cff@siscom.net
Web: www.cffinc.org

**Cat Federation
of Southern Africa**
P.O. Box 25
Bromhof 2125
Rep. of South Africa
Phone or Fax: +27 11 867-4318
E-mail: webmaster@cfsa.co.za
Web: www.cfsa.co.za

Federation Internationale Feline
Ms. Penelope Bydlinski
Little Dene
Lenham Heath
Maidstone, Kent
GB-ME17 2BS
Phone: +44 1622 850913
Fax: +44 1622 850908
E-mail: penbyd@compuserve.com
Web: www.fife.org

Federazione Italiana Associazioni Feline
c/o Rag. Cesare Ghisi
Via Carlo Poma n.20
46100—Mantova, Italy
Phone: 0376-224600
Fax: 0376-224041
E-mail: fiafmn@mynet.it
Web: www.zero.it/fiaf

**The Feline Control
Council of Victoria, Inc.**
Royal Melbourne Showgrounds
Epsom Road, Ascot Vale,
Victoria 3032, Australia
Phone: (03) 9281 7404
Fax: (03) 9376 2973
E-mail: m.jones@rasv.metbourne.net
Web: www.hotkey.net.au/ -fccvic

**Governing Council
of the Cat Fancy**
4-6 Penel Orlieu
Bridgwater, Somerset,
TA6 3PG. (UK)
Phone: +44 (0) 1278 427 575
E-mail: GCCF_CATS@compuserve.com
Web: ourworld. compuserve.com/
homepages/GCCF_CATS/
welcome.htm#office

**International
Cat Exhibitors, Inc.**
P.O. Box 772424
Coral Springs, FL 33077-2424
Web: members.aol.com/
jhagercat/ICE.htm

The International Cat Association, Inc.
P.O. Box 2684
Harlingen, TX 78551
Phone: 956-428-8047
Fax: 956-428-8047
E-mail: ticaeoe@xanadu2.net
Web: www.tica.org

Ocicats International
c/o Alana DeBruhl
94 Timberwild Court
Canton, NC 28716
Phone: 818-648-7953

United Feline Organization
218 NW 180th Street
Newberry, FL 32669
Phone and Fax: 352-472-3253
Email: UFO1FL@worldnet.att.net
Web: www.aracnet.com/ -ltdltd/
ufo.htm

World Cat Federation
Hubertstraße 280
D-45307 Essen, Germany
Phone: +49 201/555724
Fax: +49 201/509040
E-mail: wcf@nrw-online.de
Web: home.nrw-online.de/wcf/english/
ehome.html

Index